HOW THEY LIVED

A SOLDIER IN WORLD WAR I

STEWART
ROSS

Illustrated by
John Haysom

Wayland

HOW THEY LIVED

Editor: Amanda Earl

First published in 1987 by
Wayland (Publishers) Limited
61 Western Road, Hove
East Sussex BN3 1JD, England

© Copyright 1987 Wayland (Publishers) Limited

All words that appear in **bold**
in the text are explained in the
glossary on page 31.

British Library Cataloguing in Publication Data
Ross, Stewart
A soldier in World War I. – (How they lived)
1. World War, 1914–1918   2. Soldiers –
History – 20th century
I. Title   II. Haysom, John   III. Series
940.4'83   V767
ISBN 1 85210 198 9

Typeset by Kalligraphics Limited, Redhill, Surrey
Printed and bound in Belgium by Casterman S.A.

CONTENTS

OVER THE TOP

Although it was only 5.30 in the morning, the soldiers in the trenches were already busy. Some were cleaning their rifles, while others checked their packs ready for the attack. The officers moved up and down the line encouraging their troops. Overhead, **shells** crashed and whined.

Suddenly the **bombardment** stopped. The men stood still and silent, waiting for the whistles to sound, signalling the start of the attack. When the command came the troops would have to go 'over the top', climbing out of their trenches and charging the enemy lines opposite. Few would survive, for the life of a soldier in World War I was very dangerous.

World War I lasted for over four years, from late July 1914 to November 1918. For the first time in history, the war spread all over the globe, from Russia to the Falkland Islands, and from China to the USA. However, most of the fighting took place in Europe.

On one side were the German and Austrian Empires, aided by Turkey and Bulgaria. On the other side were Russia, France and Britain, supported by small countries such as Serbia, Romania and Portugal. They were joined after the start of the war by two other major powers, the USA and Italy.

March 1915: Scottish soldiers of the Argyll and Sutherland Highlanders in the trenches.

Right *When the command came from the officers, soldiers climbed out of the trenches to begin the attack.*

4

THE SOLDIERS

Soldiers of many countries fought in World War I. Britain, for example, had a world-wide **empire** and troops from all corners of this empire came to help in the fighting. So men from Britain, Canada, Australia, New Zealand, India and Africa could all be found fighting on the same side in France. One of the toughest European campaigns, an attack on the Turkish territory of Gallipoli, was undertaken very largely by soldiers from Australia and New Zealand, known as Anzacs.

Most of the soldiers in the war

A map of the Western and Eastern Fronts, marking the major battles of the war.

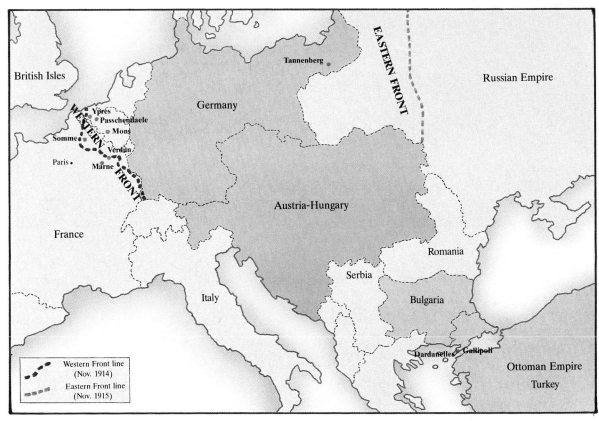

joined the **infantry**, fighting on foot. When the war broke out all armies had plenty of cavalry, but it soon became clear that a man on horseback was a very easy target for a machine gun. The **artillery** were particularly important in World War I, attracting skilled men to aim and fire the new heavy guns. The soldiers also included engineers, doctors, drivers and cooks.

Men from all corners of the British Empire came to fight in the war. These are some of Canada's troops in 1914.

Although soldiers fought in the heat of Africa and the sands of Arabia, the great majority spent the war in Europe. Most found themselves in one of the two great battle lines running across the continent, the Western and Eastern Fronts.

7

RECRUITMENT

The armies that fought in the war were huge. By 1916 the Russians had about 13½ million men in uniform. Britain had over 3¾ million in its army by the end of the war, and the armies of France and Germany were even larger.

At the outset of the war the soldiers of the British Army were all professionals, who had joined to make the army their career. This meant that the army was then quite small. Only the 100,000-strong British Expeditionary Force was immediately available in August 1914 to cross to France to stop the German attack. It soon became clear that more soldiers were needed, so there was a huge effort to get volunteers to join up.

Field Marshal Lord Kitchener was responsible for persuading ordinary citizens to sign up. Songs were written encouraging men to become soldiers and all over the country huge posters appeared showing Kitchener's face and his finger pointing, saying 'Join your country's army!' Men who didn't join up were made to feel cowardly and **unpatriotic**.

One of the many recruitment posters of World War I.

The campaign was a huge success. In the end 2½ million men and boys came forward, the largest volunteer army the world has ever seen. Some were still young teenagers.

Even this number was not enough. In 1916 Britain followed the example of other countries and introduced conscription. This meant that every able-bodied young man had to serve in the armed forces.

Kitchener's most famous poster (below) led hundreds of thousands of civilian volunteers to join the Army.

9

THE TRENCHES

For their own protection many soldiers spent a good deal of the war in trenches. These were long ditches dug in the ground, deeper than a man, with the earth piled up in front to make a protective **parapet**. The soldiers had to dig these themselves, so when they went into battle they usually carried a spade or shovel.

As the war progressed the Germans improved their trenches considerably. Their soldiers sheltered in deep con-

In the trenches, soldiers constantly watched enemy lines with the help of a periscope.

crete dug-outs, often nine metres below the battlefield. Here they were safe from bombardment and could sleep in reasonable comfort.

British soldiers had to live in trenches that were much less comfortable and secure. Often they had to dig out a space in the side of the trench for somewhere to sleep. When it rained the trenches filled with water, making them muddy and very unpleasant. Life in the trenches was uncomfortable and often **squalid**. To make the muddy, rat infested trenches seem more like home, soldiers gave them the names of London landmarks, such as Marble Arch and Westminster Bridge.

In the front of his trench the British soldier cut a firing step, on which he could stand and look over the top of the parapet to fire his rifle. This was very dangerous, however, and the best way to keep an eye on the enemy was to use a **periscope**.

Above right *Irish soldiers bring food rations down the communication lines. The trenches were usually very muddy.*

Right *Soldiers often nicknamed their makeshift dug-outs to remind them of home. This one is called 'The Casino'.*

11

OFFICERS AND MEN

The soldiers of World War I were divided into the officers, who gave the commands and made the important decisions, and the fighting men. The highest officers, Field Marshals and Generals, did not come near the danger areas. They were responsible for planning campaigns and for the army's performance. When the Russians were defeated by the Germans at the Battle of Tannenberg in 1914, the Russian General Samsonov was so ashamed that he killed himself.

Junior officers shared the hardships of the **front line** with the ordinary soldiers. However, they had more secure dug-outs than the men and were looked after by servants, called batmen. The officers also had

Field Marshals plan the next offensive away from the dangers of the front line.

Junior officers shared most of the hardships of trench life. Five of the officers above were killed in the war.

better food and could usually get their clothing washed more regularly.

When an attack came, however, life for a junior officer was the most dangerous of all. He was supposed to lead the charge from the front, straight into the enemy rifle and machine gun fire. On the first day of the Battle of the Somme in 1916, three-quarters of all attacking British officers were killed or wounded. In all, 20,000 British soldiers were killed and 40,000 injured on that one day.

Many of the young volunteer officers were close to their men, who both liked and respected them. The British awarded special new decorations – the Military Cross, for bravery by junior officers, and the Military Medal for soldiers who showed exceptional bravery in battle.

DAILY ROUTINE

Life in the trenches was unhealthy and often dangerous. But for most of the time it was just very boring. Night was the most testing time, for then soldiers made raids over the ground between their trenches and the enemy's front lines. This area was known as no-man's-land

Between bombardments, there was little to do apart from playing cards and reading.

Soldiers sorting letters from home – an important link with the outside world.

Canadian soldiers wait their turn for the daily routine of shaving.

because it belonged to neither of the armies. In cold, damp and uncomfortable conditions, most soldiers slept in the trenches for little more than four hours. A sentry found asleep at his post was shot.

Dawn was the most common time for an attack. Once it had passed, the men could 'stand down' and relax. After a meagre breakfast there were a number of jobs to be done, such as repairing the trench after a bombardment, or cleaning equipment. The daily medical check was another feature of life in the trenches.

For much of the day men in the front line sat around reading, smoking or playing cards. Letters home had to be read by a **censor** before they were sent, and information that might upset those at home, or be of use to the enemy was crossed out.

Occasionally the enemy would start a bombardment. When this happened soldiers had to keep their heads down and hope that they were not hit. On Christmas Day, 1914, British and German troops left their trenches and played football together. But this was strongly disapproved of by the authorities and was never done again.

WEAPONS

Most soldiers in World War I carried a rifle. This could kill a person up to 1½ km away. With a sharp bayonet fitted beneath the barrel, it also became an effective weapon for close fighting. Each rifle carried several bullets in a **magazine** for rapid fire, but the machinery had to be kept clean if it was to work efficiently. Soldiers going into attack were also armed with hand-held bombs, called hand grenades.

The best defensive weapon was the machine gun, which could fire many shots in rapid succession. In 1914 this was still quite a new device and the British army had very few. But it soon became clear that this was the weapon to decide the outcome of the war, and both sides produced as

Australian Anzacs loading a trench mortar. The shell of this gun was nicknamed 'the flying pig'.

many as they could. A soldier manning a well-sited machine gun could hold hundreds of men at bay. A burst of fire from one of these machine guns could cut a man in half.

The soldiers met other new weapons. The most deadly was poisonous gas. Some gases affected the lungs when inhaled, so soldiers were issued with gas masks. Another gas, known as 'mustard' gas, caused terrible burns and even blindness. However, using these gases was also dangerous, for the wind could blow them in the wrong direction.

Above *The machine gun was a new and vital weapon in World War I.*

Below *Soldiers often wore masks to protect themselves from 'mustard' gas.*

FOOD

Feeding the millions of soldiers in the front lines was not at all easy. The Russians were the least efficient and at times their men were so hungry that they were unable to fight. German supplies were better organized, but by the end of the war even their men were going hungry be-

Soldiers eating their rations during the Battle of the Somme. Food was dull and unvaried with few fresh vegetables.

cause the British Navy was stopping food ships getting to German ports.

British soldiers did not often go hungry, but they found their meals dull. Most of the food arrived in tins. One of the more popular cans contained 'maconochie', a mixture of meat and vegetable stew, also known as a 'dinner in a tin'. There was also plenty of corned beef, cheese, bread, jam and biscuits but fresh fruit and vegetables were rare.

Supplies had to be brought up to the front line by lorry, or horse and cart, then carried by men along the communication trenches. If one of these was hit the troops in the front line went hungry until more supplies could get through.

A cup of tea was an important part of life in the trenches, although it rarely tasted like that of home!

Some examples of the tinned food supplied during the war. Dried biscuits (bottom right) were popular with jam.

The favourite drink of the soldiers was tea and there was always plenty brewing. However, it did not always taste very pleasant. Water was even more difficult to get to the front line than food, for it was very heavy to carry, and foul-tasting chemicals were added to purify it. To get round this soldiers collected rainwater, or melted ice and snow in winter.

19

CLOTHING

By the time of World War I almost all armies had done away with the splendid but impractical uniforms of the nineteenth century. Instead, soldiers wore **camouflaged** clothing, usually **khaki**-coloured. The only exceptions to this were the Arab forces fighting against the Turks in the desert, who wore traditional robes.

When fighting, most soldiers wore

Left *A soldier's uniform was practical and designed to fit in with the surroundings.*

In the stifling hot weather at Gallipoli, Australian soldiers wore only their shorts.

In the desert war with the Turks, Captain Lawrence (Lawrence of Arabia) found the traditional Arab robes cooler than the British uniform.

Troops came to fight in World War I from all over the British Empire. An Indian soldier's battledress was quite similar to the British uniform.

steel helmets to protect their heads. Their tough, practical jackets were ideal for the winter but much too hot in the summer. In the stifling heat of the Gallipoli trenches, the Anzac troops wore shorts and discarded their heavy battledress tops.

In attack every soldier carried a pack. This contained all that was essential for survival: food, water, a blanket, first aid, ammunition and a waterproof cape. When a man was carrying his heavy pack as well as a rifle, bombs and a spade, it was very difficult to advance quickly and he soon became tired.

The bottoms of a soldier's trousers were fastened with bandage-type leggings to stop them flapping about. On his feet he wore stout leather boots. Unfortunately these were not waterproof, and for much of their time in the trenches soldiers had to live with soaking wet feet.

IN THE WINTER

Soldiers hated the winter more than any other time of the year. For those in the trenches of the Western Front it meant long, dark and dangerous nights, rain and endless mud. In some parts of the battlefield the mud was so deep that men drowned, and even horses were known to sink into it. These conditions were caused by the endless bombardment of heavy artillery, which destroyed all canals and ditches, and churned up the land.

During the winter months men in the front line found it almost impossible to get dry. Not only were their feet wet from slopping about in the muddy trenches, but after a while

Soldiers found it very difficult to keep warm in the bitter winter conditions.

22

their clothing too became completely soaked through.

The cold was worst on the Russian front. The German attack of 1915 was halted by the severe winter weather. Sentries were found frozen to death in the morning. Lorries and trains would not work, and guns quickly became iced up.

When snow lay on the ground, dark army uniforms stood out, making the soldiers easier targets for enemy **snipers**. Nevertheless, on the Eastern Front more soldiers died from disease and exposure to the harsh weather than from the fighting.

Soldiers' clothes were constantly damp in the freezing cold dug-outs.

Endless rain and snow made the front line very muddy.

ON LEAVE

Soldiers could not live at the front line for more than a few weeks without rest. When their turn came the men made their way down the communication trenches to safe camps behind the lines. Here they could sleep, change into clean clothes, take a bath and relax. In the summer, if the guns were not firing, they could lie in the sunshine and try to forget the horrors of the war.

Soldiers kept their spirits up by singing songs. Many of these expressed a wish to leave the war and go home. 'It's a long way to Tipperary' was one such song. In another they sang, 'Take me over the sea, where whizzbangs can't get at me'. A

Safely behind the battle lines, soldiers take a well deserved rest and try to forget about the war.

'whizzbang' was slang for a shell.

Every now and again soldiers were allowed home on leave. These times were a strange mixture of happiness and misery. The men were delighted to be at home and they enjoyed themselves in the pubs, music halls and theatres. But all the time they knew that soon they had to bid farewell to their loved ones again, and return to the terrible trenches.

Above *1916: Wounded soldiers enjoy themselves at a dinner given in their honour at the Savoy Hotel, London.*

Below *Soldiers meet at Victoria Station, London, ready to return to the Front after time on leave. Such occasion were very sad.*

ATTACK

Before every attack the artillery bombarded the enemy as heavily as they could. The British shelled the German lines for a week before the Battle of the Somme. This was done to break up the enemy defences and was called 'softening them up' ready for an attack.

By the end of the war, advances by foot soldiers were always supported by aircraft and tanks. But until late in 1917 an attack meant thousands of infantrymen charging the enemy positions. In the days before an attack, engineers dug tunnels beneath enemy trenches. These

were then filled with explosives which were set off when the attack began. At night, **patrols** crept out into no-man's-land and tried to cut the enemy's barbed wire to make it easier for the advancing troops to get through.

Once the whistles had signalled for the start of an attack and the troops had clambered out of their trenches, anything could happen. Some men managed to make their way through the hail of bullets to the enemy lines. Here tough hand-to-hand fighting took place. Behind them, strewn over the battlefield, their colleagues lay dead and wounded. An advance of only 8 km in the late summer of 1917 cost the British 244,897 casualties. Not surprisingly, every soldier dreaded being told that he was going to take part in an attack.

The noise of shellfire, the hail of bullets and the choking smoke made every attack terrifying.

Medical treatment at the front line was very basic. The main fear was that wounds would become infected in the dirty conditions. Sadly, those soldiers injured in 'no-man's-land' between the trenches and enemy line, could not usually be rescued.

MEDICAL SERVICES

The living conditions for most soldiers were very unhealthy. Epidemics swept through the trenches, spread by germs in dirty food and drink. **Dysentery**, **cholera** and **typhus** were common diseases, but even influenza could kill a man weakened by poor diet and lack of sleep.

There were no adequate toilets in the trenches, and not enough water for washing. The smell of a trench in the summer was ghastly, made worse by the stench of rotting bodies. Rats thrived, frequently running over men as they slept. Many soldiers were infested with **lice**.

Wounded soldiers were not always given proper medical treatment. If a man was hit in no-man's-land he usually had to lie there until he died, unless he was able to drag himself back to his own lines. At night the cries of the wounded were terrible.

There were no antibiotics at the time of World War I. Because it was difficult to clean wounds and sterilize instruments, **gangrene** was common. Worst of all, perhaps, was 'shell-shock'. A soldier suffering from this would break down, unable to stand the strain of war and he would be sent home. Many never recovered.

Stretcher-bearers struggle with an injured soldier in the mud at the front line.

PEACE

The fighting on the Western Front finally stopped at 11 o'clock on the morning of 11 November 1918. The Germans had asked for a cease-fire because the nation was exhausted and could no longer go on fighting. Gradually the soldiers returned home and tried to take up their normal lives again. But they would never forget what they had been through.

No one knows exactly how many soldiers died in World War I. The number is probably about 10 million, or 300 every hour of the war. A soldier's life is always hard, but no soldiers have ever had so terrible a time as those who fought in World War I.

A cemetery of just some of the young British soldiers killed in France. After World War I, people began to realize that a whole generation of men had been wasted on the battlefield – often for no better purpose than to gain a few metres of land.

GLOSSARY

Artillery An army's heavy guns.
Bombardment A long attack with heavy guns.
Camouflaged Made to look like the surroundings.
Censor Someone who cuts out information from a letter, which may have been of use to the enemy.
Cholera A lethal disease caused by consuming dirty water or food.
Dysentery An seriously infectious disease causing diarrhoea.
Empire Land in different parts of the world ruled by one country.
Front Line The line along which an army fights.
Gangrene A very serious complaint, caused by lack of blood to a part of the body, resulting in poisoning.
Infantry Foot soldiers.

Khaki The green-brown camouflage colours of an army uniform.
Lice A wingless blood-sucking insect.
Magazine A store of bullets, shells or explosives.
Parapet A low wall.
Patrol A small group of soldiers who undertake a particular task.
Periscope A system of mirrors for seeing over the trench parapet.
Shell An exploding bomb fired by a gun.
Sniper A rifle marksman.
Squalid Dirty and repulsive living conditions.
Typhus A severe disease causing skin rashes, a high fever and headaches.
Unpatriotic An unpatriotic person does not support his country.

MORE BOOKS TO READ

Non-fiction for younger readers

Brown, M., *Tommy Goes to War* (Dent, 1978)
Frank, Rudolf, *No Hero for the Kaiser* (Dent, 1986)
Hoare, Stephen, *Finding Out about Fighting in World War I* (Batsford, 1986)

Mair, Craig, *Britain at War 1914-1918* (Murray, 1982)
Ross, Stewart, *Lloyd George and the First World War* (Wayland, 1987)
Vincent, Adrian *A Family in World War I* (Wayland, 1987)

INDEX

Picture acknowledgements

The pictures in this book were supplied by the following: BBC Hulton Picture Library 17, 25 (top); Camera Press 8, 11 (both), 18, 19 (right); Mary Evans Picture Library 7, 13, 20, 25 (bottom); The Photo Source 21 (left), 24; Popperfoto 23 (bottom), 29; TOPHAM 4, 15 (both), 16, 21 (right), 23 (top); The artwork on page 6 is by Malcolm S. Walker and the remaining pictures are from the Wayland Picture Library.